From Bud to Blossom

by

Gail Saunders-Smith

Pebble Books

an imprint of Capstone Press

Pebble Books

Pebble Books are published by Capstone Press
818 North Willow Street, Mankato, Minnesota 56001
http://www.capstone-press.com
Copyright © 1998 by Capstone Press

Library of Congress Cataloging-in-Publication Data
Saunders-Smith, Gail.
  From bud to blossom/by Gail Saunders-Smith.
    p. cm.
  Includes bibliographical references (p. 23) and index.
  Summary: Simple text and photographs describe the stage in
the life cycle of apples when the buds on a tree turn into leaves
and apple blossoms.
  ISBN 1-56065-583-6
  1. Apples--Development--Juvenile literature. [1. Apples.]
I. Title.

SB363.S286 1998   ᒍ
571.8'2373--dc21   63 4. 11   97-29798
                        5 A U   CIP
                        C . 1   AC

Editorial Credits

Lois Wallentine, editor; Timothy Halldin and James Franklin,
design; Michelle L. Norstad, photo research

Photo Credits

John Marshall Outdoor Photography, 4, 8
Mark Turner, cover, 10
Unicorn Stock/ Ronald E. Partis, 6; Martha McBride, 12, 14, 16;
  Judy Hile, 1, 18; Marshall Prescott, 20

Table of Contents

4

Apple trees have leaf buds.

6

Leaf buds open up.

8

Leaf buds
become leaves.

Apple trees have apple buds.

12

Apple buds open up.

14

Apple buds become blossoms.

Apple trees have apple blossoms.

Apple blossoms
open up.

Apple blossoms will become apples.

Words to Know

bud—a small shoot on a plant that grows into a leaf or a flower

blossom—a flower on a fruit tree or other plant that becomes a fruit or vegetable

leaf—a flat and usually green part of a plant

Read More

Burckhardt, Ann L. *Apples.* Mankato, Minn.: Bridgestone Books, 1996.

Gibbons, Gail. *The Seasons of Arnold's Apple Tree.* San Diego: Harcourt Brace Jovanovich, 1984.

Micucci, Charles. *The Life and Times of the Apple.* New York: Orchard Books, 1992.

Internet Sites

All About Apples
http://www.dole5aday.com/about/apple/ apple1.html

Apple Bud Stages
http://orchard.uvm.edu/AIM/ aimbudstage/default.html

Apple Facts: How Do You Grow Apples?
http://www.pref.aomori.jp/nourin/ringo/ rin-e06.html

Note to Parents and Teachers

This book illustrates the life cycle stages of an apple tree from leaf buds to apple blossoms. The clear photographs support the beginning reader in making and maintaining the meaning of the text. The nouns and verbs are repeated several times before changing. The sentence structure is repeated, providing a supportive pattern. Children may need assistance in using the Table of Contents, Words to Know, Read More, Internet Sites, and Index/Word List sections of the book.

Index/Word List

Word Count: 40